W9-DFH-556

Top Secret

Undercover Agents

Jil Fine

HIGH
interest
books

Children's Press®
A Division of Scholastic Inc.
New York / Toronto / London / Auckland / Sydney
Mexico City / New Delhi / Hong Kong
Danbury, Connecticut

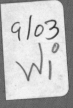

d Michelle Innes

Photo Credits: Cover © Eyewire; p. 5 © Brownie Harris/Corbis; pp. 7, 12 © Bettmann/Corbis; pp. 8–9 © Hulton-Deutsch Collection/Corbis; p. 11 © North Wind Picture Archives; pp. 14–15, 17, 37, 38–39 © AP/Wide World Photos; p. 18 ©Bob Daemmrich/The Image Works; p. 21 © Philadelphia Daily News/Jim MacMillan/The Image Works; p. 25 © AFP/Corbis; pp. 27, 29 © Everett Collection; p. 30 © Photodisc; p. 33 © Brian Bailey/Corbis; p. 34 © Steve Starr/Corbis; p. 40 © Alan Schein Photography/Corbis

Library of Congress Cataloging-in-Publication Data

Fine, Jil.
    Undercover agents / Jil Fine.
    p. cm. — (Top secret)
    Summary: Provides a history of undercover police work, particularly in the United States, and looks at the preparations made before an undercover operation as well as differences between light and deep cover. Includes bibliographical references and index.
    ISBN 0-516-24315-2 (lib. bdg.) — ISBN 0-516-24378-0 (pbk.)
    1. Undercover operations—United States—Juvenile literature. 2. Criminal investigation—United States—Juvenile literature. 3. Police—United States—Juvenile literature. [1. Undercover operations. 2. Criminal investigation. 3. Police.] I. Title. II. Top secret (New York, N.Y.)

HV8080.U5 F38 2003
363.2'32—dc21

                                                    2002008596

Contents

Introduction

The exciting, yet dangerous, world of undercover police agents is often the basis of novels, TV shows, movies, and even video games. However, real-life police undercover work is no game. Undercover agents go where uniformed police officers cannot go. They work long hours—often in uncomfortable and dangerous situations—gathering information. The information they gather is used to help put criminals in jail. Undercover agents handle many types of crime including auto theft, Internet crime, and international drug trafficking. Sometimes an undercover agent's assignment can last for several months or even a year.

Undercover work is risky because undercover agents must get close to criminals. Sometimes undercover agents must pose as a criminal's friend to gather information. Undercover agents must guard their true identities carefully. One wrong move could mean blowing their cover and their safety!

Many undercover police agents must move in the fast lane of the criminal world to track down car thieves.

This book will take you behind the scenes into the dangerous world of police undercover agents. You will learn what it takes to be an undercover agent. You will also learn some of the methods used by agents to fight crime. Let's enter the world of police undercover agents right now!

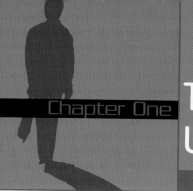

Chapter One
The History of Police Undercover Agents

It may be hard to believe, but the earliest undercover agents were criminals. Around 1800, François Vidocq escaped from a French jail. He had been jailed for fighting. In fact, Vidocq escaped from jail several times. Every time the police arrested him, Vidocq found a way to escape. Finally, Vidocq made a deal with the police. He would work for them, sharing his knowledge of the criminal world to help catch criminals and solve crimes. In return, the police agreed to clear his criminal record. Vidocq's assignment was to temporarily return to jail as a police spy. He gave police the information that other prison inmates had told him. This information helped the French police recapture prisoners who had escaped from jail.

In 1810, Vidocq started a criminal investigation unit for the French police. Most of the detectives in this unit were former criminals. This system of using

François Vidocq spent twenty-one months in jail gathering information for the French police.

England created its first lasting police force in 1829 in London. Police officers were called "bobbies" after the first leader of the police department, Sir Robert Peel.

a criminal to catch a criminal was also used in England. In 1842, the police in London, England, started their own undercover agency called the Criminal Investigation Division.

Police in the United States

In 1845, New York City officially created the first police department in the United States. It was modeled after the London Metropolitan Police

CLASSIFIED INFORMATION

In 1836, the police in New York City started using plainclothes, or out-of-uniform, police officers. These early police undercover agents were nicknamed "Shadows" by citizens. Shadows went undercover in crowds at parades and other public events to arrest criminals, such as pickpockets.

Department. Like London's police department, the New York City Police Department used a military-like chain of command. The policy of setting up local police departments spread quickly throughout the country. In ten years, most cities in the United States had organized police departments. However, uniformed police officers were not able to go undercover. This meant that police officers were only able to catch criminals in the act of committing a crime, or sometimes after the crime was committed. This made it nearly impossible to prevent a crime before it happened.

The Pinkertons and Beyond

The 1800s were a time of great change in the United States. Many people moved west, seeking a better way of life. New towns were being built. New businesses, such as banks and stores, were started to meet the needs of people. Trains and stagecoach lines spread across the country. However, many new towns did not have a way to stop unlawful behavior. Criminals often robbed banks, trains, stagecoaches, and other businesses.

Train robberies were common in the 1800s. Many victims were stripped of their life savings by dangerous outlaws.

In 1850, Allan Pinkerton, a former Chicago detective, started the Pinkerton National Detective Agency. At first, Pinkerton's private agency specialized in preventing train robberies. Pinkerton agents often worked undercover. Sometimes they posed as criminals and joined gangs of robbers. Pinkerton agent Charles Siringo successfully caught members of Butch Cassidy's Wild Bunch. The Wild Bunch was a group of criminals who robbed banks and trains. In time, the

Allan Pinkerton led the charge in the United States for a new way of fighting crime that used undercover agents.

agency stopped other criminal activity, such as counterfeiting. The Pinkerton National Detective Agency was very successful. Its success showed U.S. law-enforcement authorities that undercover agents could be a strong tool in the fight against crime.

As industry grew and more people moved to cities, so did crime. In the early 1900s, the New York City Police

Department started undercover squads to fight crime in the many different ethnic neighborhoods in the city. Each undercover squad was staffed with agents who were of the same ethnic background as the community they worked in. These undercover operations were successful in preventing and controlling crime.

Police also started using informants to get information. Informants are people who know something valuable about the criminals who are being investigated. In return for the information they provided to the police, the informants were often paid or were not punished for crimes that they had committed.

CLASSIFIED INFORMATION

The symbol of the Pinkerton agency was an eye. The term *private eye* comes from their symbol. The eye was meant to show that the Pinkerton agents were always looking for criminals.

When people are angry about events in their town or country they sometimes stage protest marches. Undercover police mix in with crowds to keep people from starting trouble.

Undercover police work remained much the same until the 1960s. The 1960s were a time of social and political unrest. Many Americans were unhappy with the U.S. government. There were many rallies and marches where people protested important issues. Some people, however, showed their dissatisfaction by setting off bombs or rioting. Undercover agents were often used to prevent these crimes. In the 1960s,

many police departments used undercover agents to investigate violent political groups.

Today, advanced technology has made it possible for undercover agents to gather information more effectively than ever before. They can secretly listen to phone conversations and even conduct photo surveillance from very far distances. To prevent crime, agents often take on new identities. They pretend to be drug dealers, assassins, or even ordinary citizens. Undercover police work is not a job for the timid. It takes a person who is willing to work hard and take risks. It also takes special training.

Chapter Two

Taking Off the Uniform

Working in plainclothes is important for undercover police detectives in their fight against crime. All detectives work in plainclothes. This allows them to go places and learn things that a uniformed officer might not. Sometimes police officers on patrol also work in plainclothes to blend in with the crowd. A plainclothes officer is more likely to witness a crime because people don't know that he or she is a police officer.

Undercover agents work in local and state police departments. There are undercover operations in many different fields. Most undercover operations involve drug trafficking. Other operations may investigate stolen property, illegal gun sales and purchases, and Internet crimes.

Undercover police agents take aim at illegal gun sales. Agents try to buy firearms from gun stores without showing the proper paperwork. If a store owner breaks the law and sells the agent a gun, legal action may be taken.

Before they become police officers, police cadets spend a lot of time learning in the classroom. There they are taught the laws that they will uphold and the techniques that they will use to fight crime.

Just Starting Out

In order to be an undercover agent, you must first become a police officer. To become a police officer in most police departments, you must be at least twenty-one years old and a high school graduate. Some police departments require two years of college or military service. Before joining the police department, you must pass a written test. In addition, you must pass medical, psychological, and physical agility exams. Police officer cadets must also pass a background check. Before becoming a police officer, cadets go through at least twelve weeks of training. They learn many things, including how to deal with the public and how to handle dangerous criminals. High school graduates that are younger than twenty-one can usually get a job with a police department before they join. They work in the police department offices and can take classes to prepare to become police officers.

It is best for an officer to be experienced with police work before going undercover. An inexperienced officer may not be able to deal with problems that come up when doing undercover work. An undercover agent should be a good investigator and be able to communicate well with others. He or she must be able to handle stressful situations without panicking. All undercover agents must volunteer for undercover duty. An undercover operation could be very unsafe for an agent who didn't want to be there in the first place.

Sometimes, new officers are perfect for undercover work. This is because they don't yet look or act like police officers. New officers may also fit a certain physical description that is needed in an operation. For example, if the police department wants an officer to work undercover in a high school, a thirty-year-old officer would not blend in very well!

The Chosen Ones

Once an officer is chosen to work undercover, he or she must be trained. Undercover training can last from just a few days to a month. Officers may go to

Young police trainees, such as these, work hard to become effective undercover agents of the future.

several training classes to learn about different kinds of undercover work. This includes such things as investigation and surveillance techniques, how to plan an operation, how to create a false identity, and how to deal with stress. If the officers are working to break up narcotics trafficking, they will have to know what different drugs look like. They also need to know the name that each drug is called on the street. Officers must also know the laws that they have to obey when working undercover. If officers break a law while gathering evidence, they might not be able to use that evidence in court. When this happens, an entire undercover operation could be wasted and the criminals set free.

What's the Plan?

Before an undercover agent can start an operation, a plan must be made. Part of this plan is creating the agent's undercover identity. If an agent is going undercover for a long time, an entirely new life may have to be created for him or her. Fake forms of identification, such as a driver's license or social security number, may be made. An agent may be given a new place to live to protect his or her undercover identity. Many criminals check people's backgrounds before doing business with them. If an agent does not have a good background story—and the documents to prove it—the agent's cover may be blown. Sometimes undercover agents even stage a showdown with other police officers to prove to the criminals that they are not police officers.

It's important that the undercover operation is planned and that all involved stick to the plan. Undercover agents are never alone on an operation. They always have a supervisor. The supervisor is responsible for communicating with the undercover agent. Supervisors must know when and where all meetings with the criminal suspect are being held. During longer operations, the agent checks in with his or her supervisor about once a day. In the case of possible danger to an agent, the supervisor is responsible for calling off the operation or sending in backup officers to help. The supervisor also chooses what technology and what vehicles to use for surveillance.

Under Surveillance

There are many different kinds of devices that undercover agents can use during their operations. Hidden video cameras, wiretaps, and electronic bugs are all used by police to catch criminals. Agents may use night vision goggles, heat sensors, and other devices to spy on criminals. However, many criminals also use equipment such as electronic bugs and wiretap detectors to find out if an agent is spying on them. Technology advances quickly. The police must keep up with the many new devices on the market so that they can compete with criminals.

Since undercover work can be very dangerous, most undercover agents wear bulletproof vests for protection. As we've seen, however, criminals are aware of the devices used by police. They may arrange drug deals to take place indoors, often in a dealer's apartment. Undercover agents may be searched before entering the apartment. This means that the agents can't wear a bulletproof vest or other device that might save his or her life because

Smile! You're on a police surveillance camera! Police agents in cities around the world use cameras to watch streets and buildings looking for danger.

the criminal might find it. Agents have to make the difficult decision to either wear a vest or risk being found out. Many agents have lost their lives while working undercover.

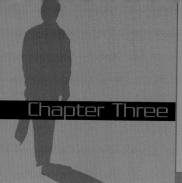

Chapter Three

Going Undercover

Undercover agents may work in either deep-cover or light-cover operations. In deep-cover operations, an agent creates a new identity and enters into the criminal world. The agent lives out the undercover role. He or she may have a new home, job, and car for the operation. Many agents who work deep undercover will become friends with criminals. Their job is to gather evidence that may one day be used against their new "friends." Deep-cover operations can last for several years! Deep-cover work can also be very stressful. Because of the amount of stress undercover agents experience, they get more time off than regular police officers.

Deep Cover

Deep-cover agents are usually not from the city or town where their assigned operation takes place.

Actors Johnny Depp (left) and Al Pacino (right) starred in the movie *Donnie Brasco*. The movie told the true story of an undercover agent who spent years spying on people involved in organized crime.

Agents would be putting their lives on the line if they ran into someone whom they had once arrested. Undercover agents commonly work with informants to find, and enter, the criminal world. For example, an informant may introduce an agent into a group as the person he or she is dating. The undercover agent and the informant will pretend to date, then pretend to break up. During this time, the agent meets many people and works to find out which criminal is in charge. The more people the agent meets, the more arrests may be made. It is possible to get dozens of arrests out of one undercover investigation.

While the agent is working undercover, he or she has to be careful not to be discovered. Sometimes the agent is asked to prove that he or she is part of the criminal world. Some drug dealers even insist that the people they deal with take the illegal drugs in front of them to be sure they are not police officers. If possible, the agent will try to talk his or her way out of taking the drugs. However, it is not always possible. If the agent's life is in danger, he or she may be forced to take the drugs. When this happens, the

The temptation for a police officer to break the law while undercover is a popular subject in movies such as *In Too Deep*, which starred actors LL Cool J (left) and Omar Epps (right).

agent is taken to a hospital or put on sick leave by the police department. Most agents strive not to break any laws while undercover.

In Too Deep

During long deep-cover operations, some agents get too involved in their new identity. They start to believe that they are the people that they are pretending to be. Many agents become close friends with the people whom they are investigating. They

Who's the undercover police officer in this picture? It could be anyone. Police send undercover agents into high schools to combat drugs and gangs.

may feel badly when they have to arrest some of their contacts in the criminal world once the investigation comes to an end. An agent may also start taking part in criminal activities. When this happens, the agent is removed from the operation as soon as possible. Some agents even have problems getting back into regular police work when the operation has ended. Most get some time off before going back to uniformed police work.

Working With Others

Many times, state and local police work with the Federal Bureau of Investigation (FBI). In 1992, the FBI, the New York City Police Department, and other law enforcement agencies worked together to catch people who had been stealing airline tickets. They set up an undercover travel agency to attract thieves. The operation resulted in the arrest of sixty people.

Going It Alone

Some police departments send undercover agents into local schools to find illegal drug use. The Los Angeles Police Department started the School Buy program in 1974. The School Buy program places undercover agents in local high schools for a semester. Before the operation begins, an agent drives around the campus of the school to which he or she is assigned. He or she looks at how the students are dressed and how they act. During the operation, the agent goes to classes every day like a normal student. He or she tries to find out who are the drug dealers. In one year, agents in the School Buy program arrested 136 drug dealers.

Under Light Cover

Light-cover operations are used for shorter periods of time. The agent usually can return to his or her real home and family at the end of each day. An agent who works in light cover may have to use a different name, but he or she does not usually need a very detailed cover story. There are many different types of light-cover operations. For example, an officer may leave a wallet hanging out of his or her pocket. If someone tries to steal the wallet, he or she is arrested. In many cities, police also go undercover as a drunken or homeless person.

In other light-cover operations, an officer may go to a place where a criminal is known to attack people. For instance, if people are getting attacked while jogging, an undercover officer, dressed like a jogger, will go running in the area where the attacks are happening. Once the attacker strikes, he or she will be arrested by the undercover officer. Undercover agents have also worked in nursing homes and doctors' offices to catch workers who abuse patients.

Undercover police are always on the go.
Posing as a jogger is just one of the
many ways they catch criminals.

The Buy and Bust

Another common light-cover operation involves an agent pretending to be a drug buyer. The agent arranges to meet a drug dealer. When the agent is with the drug dealer, two plainclothes officers will walk by to make sure everything is going as planned. Once the agent pays for the drugs, at least five officers, who were hidden nearby, come to make the arrest. About five thousand of these operations happen every year!

Teamwork is very important in undercover work. When an officer is ready to make an arrest, he or she gives a signal to other officers who rush the suspect. This teamwork decreases the chances of anyone getting hurt during a struggle.

Obeying the Law

Undercover agents must follow the law just like uniformed police officers. Doing so protects the rights of both innocent people and criminals. Police cannot put someone under surveillance without a good reason. Agents must get a warrant before starting a wiretap on someone. The undercover agent's goal is to make an arrest. While undercover, the agent must gather evidence that will be used to get a warrant for an arrest. Sometimes, agents go too far in trying to get evidence to arrest someone. If agents force or trick someone into committing a crime, the agent commits entrapment. Entrapment is illegal. The tricked person may not have committed the crime without the agents' actions. Undercover agents have to be careful not to commit a crime while they are trying to catch others.

Sometimes a police officer may be the person being investigated in an undercover operation. If a police department learns of a police officer mistreating people, undercover agents may be used to investigate the officer. Undercover agents are often used to investigate corruption, or illegal activities, within a police department, too.

Chapter Four

On the Lookout

Since the terrorist attacks of September 11, 2001, fighting terrorism has been a major concern for law-enforcement agencies in the United States. Local police departments often act as the eyes and ears of the FBI. Police departments in major cities, such as New York and Los Angeles, have anti-terrorist divisions. Police departments in California, Florida, Maryland, Illinois, and other states also have anti-terrorist divisions. These departments work with the FBI to get information about terrorist actions. Sometimes, undercover work is needed to get a closer look at suspected terrorist groups.

The police collect information on different religious or political groups. They may decide to plant an undercover agent in a group to make sure that the group is not a terrorist threat. Since September 11, many cities have changed their laws to make it easier for police to monitor political and religious groups.

The terrorist attacks of September 11, 2001, which included an attack on the Pentagon (pictured) in Washington, D.C., left Americans shaken — and law enforcement agencies determined to prevent another attack from happening on American soil.

Protecting Privacy

While fighting terrorism is important, law-enforcement agencies must make sure that people are treated fairly. There is a danger that people who merely disagree with the police may be considered suspects. They may be arrested though they have done nothing wrong. In some cases, undercover agents have even entered a group and encouraged violence.

Technology is making it possible for the police to watch people without having to go undercover. Cameras are being used in cities and towns all over the country to watch for illegal activities. There are more than two thousand cameras watching the people of New York City. A new type of camera allows police to find criminals in a crowd. These cameras are able to measure the space between the eyes, nose, and mouth on a person's face. They then match the measurements of that face to those of known criminals. Police may

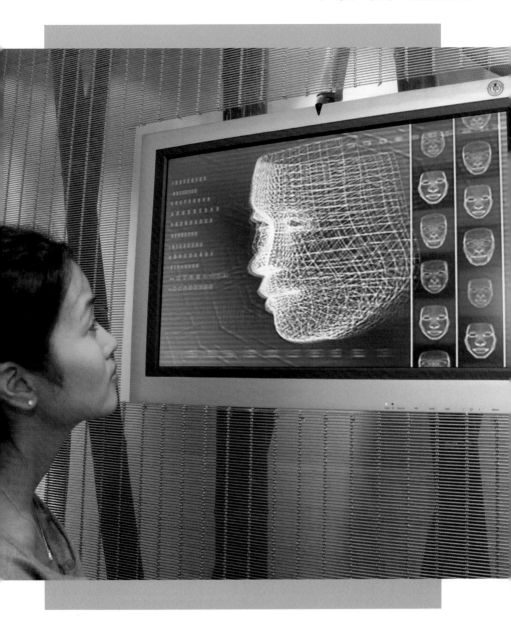

New technology, such as face recognition
↑ machines, will make fighting crime easier.

Citizens across the United States count on undercover police agents to keep them safe as they lead their daily lives.

soon have access to devices that can look through a person's clothes for guns and other dangerous objects. This technology can be very helpful for police looking to find dangerous criminals.

In the wrong hands, however, this technology can be used to spy on people who haven't broken any laws. Lawmakers and police must be careful that they protect privacy rights while still being able to catch dangerous criminals. These new technologies raise important questions. Should the police be able to watch anyone they want, even if there is no evidence that they have broken any laws? Where do we draw the line on using surveillance? The police need to make sure that in the process of catching criminals, the rights of everyday citizens are not violated.

Undercover work is dangerous. It takes well-trained people willing to risk their lives fighting crime and terrorism. Undercover operations make our world a safer place. Criminals can be caught in the act of committing a crime or before a crime can even happen.

bureau a special branch of a large
government department

counterfeiting making fake money

deep cover an undercover operation that requires an
agent to assume a new identity and live the role
for an extended period of time

detective a person who investigates crimes, usually
for or with the police

ethnic of or about a group of people with the same
race, nationality, or culture

evidence the information and facts that help prove
something or make you believe that something
is true

informant a person who gives the police information
on a criminal, usually for pay or favors

investigation the act of finding out as much as
possible about a person or crime

light cover a short-term undercover operation

operation a mission that has been carefully planned

plainclothes to be dressed in regular clothes instead of a uniform

supervisor someone who watches over and directs the work of other people

surveillance closely observing a person or group

suspect a person thought to be responsible for a crime

technology the use of science and engineering to do practical things

terrorism the use of fear or violence to reach a goal

undercover working as a spy without the knowledge of those under investigation; a secret investigation

Boraas, Tracey. *Police Detective.* Mankato, MN: Capstone Press, 2001.

Lane, Brian. *Eyewitness: Crime & Detection.* New York: Dorling Kindersley Publishing, 2000.

MccGwire, Scarlett. *Surveillance: The Impact On Our Lives.* Chatham, NJ: Raintree Steck-Vaughn, 2001.

Meltzer, Milton. *Case Closed: The Real Scoop on Detective Work.* New York: Scholastic Inc., 2001.

Thomas, Paul. *Undercover Agents.* Chatham, NJ: Raintree Steck-Vaughn, 1998.

Resources

Organizations

The American Police Hall of Fame

3801 Biscayne Boulevard
Miami, FL 33137
(305) 573-0070
Fax: (305) 573-9819
www.aphf.org

National Association of Police Organizations, Inc.

750 First Street, N.E., Suite 920
Washington, D.C. 20002
(202) 842-4420
Fax: (202) 842-4396
E-mail: napo@erols.com
www.napo.org

Web Sites

The New York City Police Museum

www.nycpolicemuseum.org

This Web site offers on-line exhibits and frequently asked questions about the history of the New York City Police Department. You will also find links to police departments and police museums in the United States and all over the world.

The Official Web Site of the Los Angeles Police Department

www.lapdonline.org

This Web site has information about the history and the different divisions of the Los Angeles Police Department. Check out the kids' section for interesting information about canine units and mounted patrol.

Index

Index

About the Author

Jil Fine is a freelance writer living in New York City.